For their generous help in offering information
and suggestions, thanks to the National Aeronautics
and Space Administration and to the Department of
Science and Technology of the New York Public Library.
Thanks, too, to Jean-Claude Landau for lucid
explanations of some basic astrophysical concepts.

The photograph of the sun on the
cover was made by a computer
from an orbiting spacecraft.

A Book
about
Planets

by BETTY POLISAR REIGOT

SCHOLASTIC BOOK SERVICES
NEW YORK • TORONTO • LONDON • AUCKLAND • SYDNEY • TOKYO

For Jeanie, Paula, and Jonathan

ISBN 0-590-31465-3

12 11 10 9 8 7 6 5 4 3 2 1   2   1 2 3 4 5 6/8

Printed in the U.S.A.

09

Contents

Introduction

Out in space, there are millions of stars with planets that go around them. The sun is one of those stars. Earth is one of the planets that goes around the sun.

Stars, like our sun, shine with their own light. Planets have no light of their own. They are lit by the light that falls on them from their star. Compared to other stars, the sun is medium size and medium bright.

We use telescopes and other special instruments to help us find out what goes on in space. We can find out about things that happened millions and billions of kilometers away and millions and billions of years ago.

Astronomers and other scientists also use computers to figure out when and where something may happen in space.

Spacecraft, loaded with instruments, are rocketed into space. They gather information to send back to Earth. They are called space probes.

Computers store many kinds of information. New information goes into the computers all the time. There will be more information by the time you finish reading this book. But some of what we already know is a good place to start.

We know that our big Earth is like a tiny speck in space.

The Solar System

Earth is one of nine planets that we know of that go around our star, the sun. Other objects — sometimes called bodies — go around the sun, too. All of these belong to our solar system.

Our solar system is in the Milky Way galaxy. There are millions of other systems in this galaxy. The Milky Way galaxy is part of the universe.

Many, many other galaxies are in the universe. We can photograph at least a billion of them with our powerful telescopes. Some are nearer to us than others.

But when we talk about outer space, "near" means billions of kilometers away!

From Earth, the other planets look flat. But they are really shaped more like balls.

Planets move in two ways. Every planet turns around and around like a spinning top. This movement is called rotating.

As each planet rotates, it also follows a path around the sun. The path is called an orbit. We say the planet orbits (revolves around) the sun.

Something else makes our solar system work the way it does. It is a force called gravity.

When we hold a pencil in our hand and let it go, it falls to the ground. The pencil falls instead of floating in air, because Earth pulls it down toward its center. The force is Earth's gravity. Earth's gravity keeps us from floating in air, too.

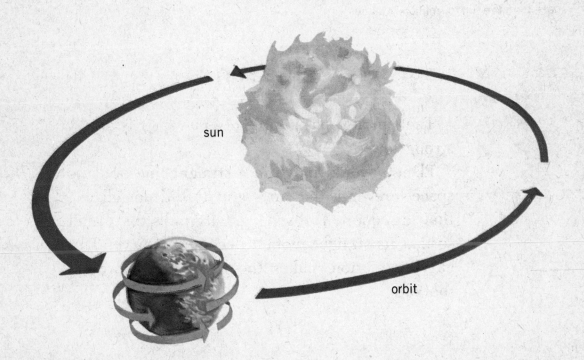

sun

orbit

Very, very hot gases shoot out into
space from the sun for millions of miles.

The sun

The sun also has a force of gravity. It is a very
strong force.

Planets would move in a straight line out into
space forever if the sun's gravity did not change
their direction. The sun's gravity pulls the planet
so that its straight motion becomes a curve. This
curving motion makes the planet orbit around
the sun.

Because of the sun's pull of gravity, all the planets in our solar system revolve around it.

The sun is a huge ball of super-hot gas. It is much bigger than Earth. The sun takes up a million times more space than Earth does.

Deep inside the sun, the temperature is hotter than the hottest furnace. The sun is so hot that it heats and lights all the planets in our solar system.

The orbits of the planets

Some planets orbit closer to the sun than others. And some are far away from the sun. The planets that are the farthest from the sun are called the outer planets.

The planets that are closer to the sun are called the inner planets. The inner planets are close to each other as well as close to the sun. There are four inner planets:

Mercury
Venus
Earth
Mars

The inner planets have a hard, rocky surface. It is possible to land a spacecraft on planets that have a hard surface.

The five outer planets are not only farther from the sun, they are also far apart from one another.

Four of them are much, much bigger than the inner planets. The four giant planets are:

Jupiter
Saturn
Uranus
Neptune

These huge planets have an icy — probably slushy — surface.

Mercury   Venus   Earth   Mars

INNER PLANETS

Jupiter

The last planet that has been discovered in our solar system is farthest away. It is Pluto. We don't know much about Pluto yet.

But we do know that it is not like the other outer planets. And it is not like the inner planets, either. Pluto is a mystery.

This is how the nine planets compare in size with one another.

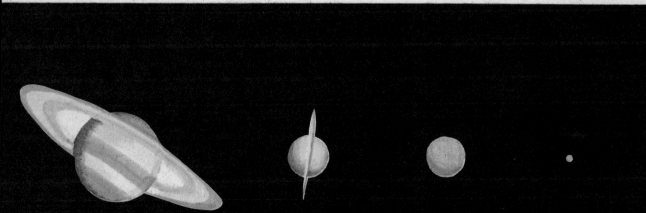

The Inner Planets

Earth

The two planets closest to the sun are Mercury and Venus. Next comes Earth. We know more about Earth than about any other planet.

Living things, as we know them, need sunlight, water, and certain gases. We know that Earth has what living things need. It has the right amount of sunlight. It has water — about three times as much water as land. And it has gases that plants and animals need to live.

Just above Earth is its atmosphere. Atmosphere is the air around an object in space. Not all objects in space have an atmosphere.

Earth does. Its atmosphere is made up mostly

This is how Earth looks from outer space.

of nitrogen and oxygen. Dust particles float inside the atmosphere. So do clouds and microbes. (Microbes are living organisms so small you need a microscope to see them.) The clouds are water droplets that form rain.

Earth has a magnetic field all around it. The magnetic field begins inside Earth's core and goes out way beyond the atmosphere. A magnetic field acts like a magnet.

Earth's atmosphere and the magnetic field above it usually stop deadly rays from the sun and other stars. The atmosphere also burns up most meteors before they can hit Earth. Earth's atmosphere and magnetic field protect life on Earth.

Scientists believe there is probably life somewhere else in the universe. But they don't know where, yet.

The planet Earth spins around — rotates — once in 24 hours. With one 24-hour rotation, most of the planet has a night and a day.

A planet rotates as if there were a long rod through its center. But there is no rod. We make believe there is and we call it an axis. The rod we call the axis always points in the direction of the North Star as Earth orbits around the sun. That is why Earth has different seasons.

During winters at the North and South Poles, the nights last much longer than they do anywhere else on the planet. A night in winter in the polar regions lasts all winter long. Summertime at the Poles is one very long day.

Earth has many kinds of climates. Temperatures on Earth can be as high as 60° Celsius (140° Fahrenheit). It gets that hot in some deserts. At the North and South Poles, it can be as cold as minus 90° Celsius (130° below zero Fahrenheit).

There may be some places on Earth where people may not be able to live. But some form of life is possible almost anywhere on Earth.

Earth's partner

The moon is Earth's natural satellite. It takes the moon 27 days and 8 hours to circle Earth. Earth and moon orbit the sun together.

The moon's surface is a lot like Earth's. But the moon has no atmosphere, no magnetic field, no water, and no sign of life.

The moon's light, like the Earth's, shines with the light of the sun. Now and then, there are certain places on the moon that seem to glow with more light. Astronomers are not sure what causes this.

Earth and moon revolve around the sun in 365 days, plus part of another day. We make up for the part of a day by adding one extra day every four years. That year is called leap year and it has 366 days.

Flying meteors make craters when they land on the moon's dry surface.

The picture on the left looks like the moon, but it's really Earth photographed from the moon.

PLANETS OF OUR SOLAR SYSTEM	How far from the sun (average distance)	How long to make one spin on its axis
Mercury	58 million kilometers (*36 million miles*)	59 Earth days
Venus	108 million km. (*67 million miles*)	243 Earth days
Earth	150 million km. (*93 million miles*)	24 Earth hours
Mars	228 million km. (*142 million miles*)	24½ Earth hours
Jupiter	778 million km. (*483 million miles*)	Just less than 10 Earth hours
Saturn	1,427 million km. (*886 million miles*)	10¼ Earth hours
Uranus	3 billion km. (*2 billion miles*)	11 Earth hours
Neptune	4½ billion km. (*3 billion miles*)	16 Earth hours
Pluto	6 billion km. (*3½ billion miles*) See footnote on page 38.	7 Earth days

How long to orbit once around the sun	Diameter*	Number of satellites
88 Earth days	4,800 kilometers (3,000 miles)	None
7½ Earth months	12,200 km. (7,600 miles)	None
1 Earth year	12,700 km. (7,900 miles)	1
23 Earth months	6,700 km. (4,200 miles)	2
12 Earth years	142,800 km. (88,000 miles)	15
29½ Earth years	120,000 km. (75,000 miles)	15-may be more
84 Earth years	51,800 km. (32,000 miles)	5
165 Earth years	49,500 km. (31,000 miles)	2
250 Earth years	3,380 km. (2,100 miles)	1

*If you went from one side of a planet, through the center to the other side, that would be the diameter.

Mercury

Mercury is the planet closest to the sun. It is also the smallest of all the known planets.

The nearby sun's glare makes it hard to see Mercury in the sky, even with a telescope.

More than three billion years ago, huge meteorites crashed into the planet. They left deep scars on its surface.

Mercury's atmosphere is much, much thinner than Earth's. There is also a very weak magnetic field around Mercury.

Mercury orbits the sun much faster than Earth does. But Mercury spins completely around on its axis much more slowly than Earth. While Mercury makes one spin, Earth has had 59 days and nights!

On Mercury, it is terribly hot and terribly cold. There is no water. There is not much atmosphere. And the gases are not the kinds living things need. Scientists say there can't be any kind of life on Mercury.

This picture of Mercury was taken with the help of a telescope on Earth.

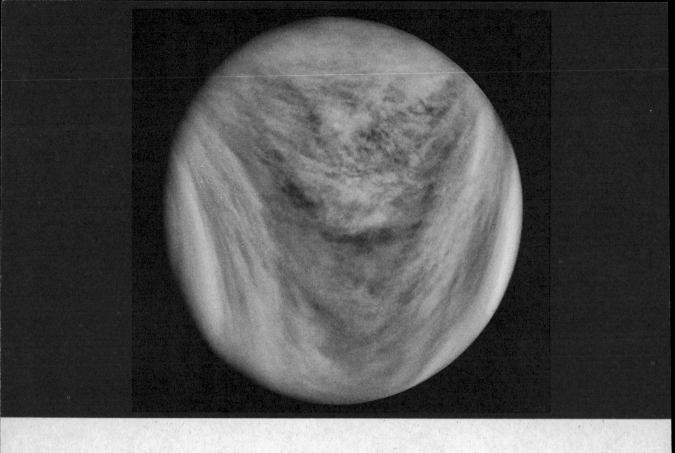

Venus

When you look up at the sky, the brightest objects you can see are the sun and the moon. The next brightest is Venus.

Venus is about the same size as Earth — just a little smaller. It is closer to Earth than any other planet. But it is very different from Earth.

Earth has lots of water, mostly in the form of oceans, rivers, and lakes. The only water we know of on Venus is in the form of water vapor. (Water vapor is a gas which you cannot see.)

Bright, yellowish clouds hide the surface of Venus.
These clouds are made of sulfur particles and
sulfuric acid.

Earth turns on its axis in 24 hours. Venus turns on its axis very slowly. Many, many days pass on Earth before Venus has a new day.

Venus' clouds swirl around fast. Winds blow at about 644 kilometers (400 miles) an hour, making wilder storms than any hurricane on Earth.

Russian scientists have landed spacecraft on Venus. Its surface is rougher than Earth's and has many more craters.

Venus is nearly twice as far from the sun as Mercury, yet it is almost as hot as Mercury. Unlike Mercury, nights and days on Venus have about the same very high temperatures.

The reason is that Venus' atmosphere has carbon dioxide gas that stays all around the planet. It's like a blanket of smog that we sometimes get over some cities on Earth.

The sun's rays come through this atmosphere and heat the planet. The planet gives off heat rays, but those rays cannot pass back through the atmosphere to outer space. The heat is trapped under the blanket of carbon dioxide gas.

Something like this happens to a car parked in the sun with the windows shut. The inside gets much hotter than the outside because heat cannot escape.

On Venus, nothing we know of can live.

Mars

Mars is the inner planet farthest from the sun. It seems a lot like Earth. Nights and days on both planets take about the same time.

Though it's a bit colder on Mars, there are clouds and fog there. And it has volcanoes, lava fields, canyons, and cracks in its crust, like Earth.

The North and South Poles also have ice caps.

Mars is called the Red Planet because its soil is red. Sand dunes, boulders, and rocks are part of the landscape. The white bar belongs to the spacecraft that landed on Mars and took the picture.

As Mars orbits, the ice cap closer to the sun shrinks because the sun's rays melt some of the ice.

About the same time each Mars year, part of the surface seems to change color. Does this mean Mars has seasons, like Earth? We don't know yet.

But there are differences between Mars and Earth. Mars has many moon-like craters, billions of years old. Its atmosphere is mostly carbon dioxide and much thinner than Earth's. Its sky is not blue, but creamy pink, because of red dust in the air.

Dust storms sometimes cover the whole planet. Water on Mars is not liquid. It's either vapor — like clouds — or ice.

And Mars has two satellites — tiny moons that revolve around it.

Many scientists think some kind of life may be possible on Mars. So far, we have no proof of it. Scientists hope to find answers with future space probes — and, someday, even with a visit from Earth people.

The Outer Planets

Except for Pluto, the outer planets are alike in a lot of ways.

They are much bigger than the inner planets.

They are mostly made of hydrogen and helium. The hydrogen and helium are in the form of gas in the planets' atmospheres. The outer planets have a lot of atmosphere.

The surface of these planets is icy — maybe slushy. And below the surface, hydrogen and helium are in a liquid form. At the center is a rocky core.

Each of these huge planets has its own system of moons.

Rings around Saturn have been seen for many years. They are probably made mostly of water, ice, or icy particles. Recently, rings have been discovered around two more giant planets — Jupiter and Uranus. Scientists expect to find a ring around Neptune, too.

Jupiter

There is a very great distance between the inner and outer planets. Jupiter, the first of the outer planets, is the largest of all the planets. Jupiter is so far away from Earth that it was hard to learn much about it, even with telescopes.

In 1979, *Voyagers 1* and *2* — United States space probes — were sent off into space from Earth. They sped through space all the way to Jupiter and sent back a lot of new information.

These spacecraft are continuing on in space. They will be sending back information from Saturn, Uranus, and possibly faraway Neptune.

These are some things we now know about Jupiter. Its outer atmosphere is very cold. But inside the planet, it gets hotter and hotter closer to the center.

Scientists do not think life is likely on Jupiter.

Jupiter spins fast on its axis. But this giant planet takes a long time to go around the sun. One Jupiter year is as long as 13 Earth years.

Fast-moving clouds whirl around Jupiter. They form a pattern like wide and narrow belts called zones and bands.

In one of these bands is a tremendous oval called the Great Red Spot. It is twice as big as Earth. Most scientists are not sure what the Great Red Spot really is. Some scientists think it may be a giant hurricane.

There is a magnetic field around Jupiter 10,000 times more powerful than Earth's.

Jupiter, the super planet, has super lightning bolts.

For hundreds of years, people could see four of Jupiter's moons through telescopes. Now we know Jupiter has at least 15 moons. They orbit Jupiter as Jupiter orbits the sun.

Astronomers expect the new information about Jupiter's moons to help explain how our solar system began, how it changed, and how Earth came to be the way it is.

The Great Red Spot looks like a big red eye. Swirling
clouds keep moving all around it.

Saturn

Beautiful Saturn, with its bright rings, is the second largest planet in our solar system. (Jupiter is the largest.) Saturn is almost 10 times bigger than Earth.

Saturn is much, much farther from the sun than Earth. It is very cold out there! And it takes almost 30 years for Saturn to go once around the sun.

Like the other very big planets, Saturn is mostly hydrogen and helium.

From far away, Saturn looks yellowish. But close-up photographs taken from the space probe, *Voyager I*, in 1980, show it has bands of different colors—pale yellow, golden brown, and reddish brown.

Saturn has many moons. Fifteen have been discovered already. The moon named Titan is one of the largest in the solar system. Titan has a lot of atmosphere.

Maybe Titan's atmosphere, like that around Venus, has kept heat from escaping into space. Maybe Titan's atmosphere and surface have stayed warm over billions of years. Maybe here is where we may find some form of life.

Here is Saturn and its famous rings. Scientists believe rings form when a satellite gets too close to the mother planet. The planet's gravity pulls the satellite apart. Particles of the satellite form rings that circle the planet.

Uranus

All the planets described so far have been known for a long, long time. Uranus was discovered only about 200 years ago by a scientist looking through a telescope.

Uranus is the third of the four big outer planets. It is a small giant — only four times bigger than Earth. It has five moons.

The orbit of Uranus is very, very far from the sun.

Uranus has nine rings. They are thin, dark, and hard to see. They were discovered while astronomers watched Uranus come close to a star. The star began to flicker before and after Uranus passed in front of it. Astronomers realized the flickering must be because Uranus has rings which were partly blocking the star's light.

It's not likely that there is life on Uranus.

Someday we hope to have pictures of Uranus and its rings. This is a drawing of how it will probably look.

When scientists studied Uranus, they found that its orbit was slightly different from what they thought it would be. They thought the difference might be due to another planet. So they looked for another planet. That's how they discovered Neptune and Pluto.

Neptune

Of the four giant planets, Neptune is farthest away from the sun. It is a very cold planet.

Neptune is a little smaller than Uranus.

It takes a little less time than Earth to rotate once. But it takes 165 Earth years for Neptune to make one orbit around the sun.

Neptune has two satellites.

Pluto

Pluto is a puzzle. It is farthest away from the sun*but it is not a giant planet. Some scientists are not sure it is a planet. Some think it may be a satellite of Neptune that was pulled away by the gravity of still another planet — another planet that has not even been discovered yet.

But whatever Pluto may be, it also has a moon that goes around it.

*Because of the way Pluto orbits, there is a time when Neptune is farther from the sun than Pluto. That is what is happening now. It happens every 228 years. By 1999, Pluto will again be the farthest planet from the sun.

This is *Columbia,* the space shuttle the United States is working on. It must be able to take off like a rocket, orbit around planets, change course in space, return to Earth, land like a plane, and be used over and over again.

What Next?

Finer and better instruments and computers are being made all the time.

Astronomers and other scientists hope some-day to have a laboratory in space and a shuttle to go back and forth from Earth to outer space. Then we can get much more information.

Men and women are being trained as as-tronauts now. Some children your age will grow up to be astronauts. Maybe you will be one of them. Maybe you will make an amazing discov-ery about life — in the universe, in the Milky Way, in our solar system, and on Earth.

Photo credits

The publisher is grateful for permission
to use the following photographs:

Freelance Photographers Guild
Pages 6–7

National Aeronautics and Space Administration
Front cover and pages 10, 15, 19, 24, 26–27,
31, 33, 35, 37, 39

Wide World Photos
Page 23

Illustrations by Ted Hanke